Land Husbandry
A Framework
for Soil and Water
Conservation

By T. F. Shaxson, N. W. Hudson, D. W. Sanders,
E. Roose, and W. C. Moldenhauer

Published in cooperation with the
World Association of Soil and Water Conservation

SOIL
AND WATER
CONSERVATION
SOCIETY

Soil and Water Conservation Society
7515 Northeast Ankeny Road
Ankeny, Iowa 50021-9764

Copyright © 1989 by the Soil and Water Conservation Society
All rights reserved
Manufactured in the United States of America

Library of Congress Catalog Card No. 89-5889

ISBN 0-935734-20-1

$12.00

Library of Congress Cataloging-in-Publication Data

Main entry under title:

Land husbandry.

"Published in cooperation with the World Association
of Soil and Water Conservation"
  Bibliography: p.
  1. Soil conservation—Handbooks, manuals, etc. 2. Hill farming—
Handbooks, manuals, etc. 3. Water conservation—Handbooks, manuals,
etc. I Shaxson, T. F. II. Soil and Water Conservation Society. III. World
Association of Soil and Water Conservation.

S623.L36 1989   631.4   89-5889
ISBN 0-935734-20-1

Contents

Preface

THE idea for this guidelines manual was conceived during the planning of a workshop held in San Juan, Puerto Rico, March 22-27, 1987. That workshop, "Soil and Water Conservation on Steep Lands," was organized by the World Association of Soil and Water Conservation and the Soil Conservation Society of America (now the Soil and Water Conservation Society). Sponsors included the U.S. Department of Agriculture's Soil Conservation Service, the U.S. Agency for International Development, and the World Resources Institute. Considerable assistance was also provided by the United Nations Food and Agriculture Organization and the Swedish International Development Authority.

The workshop drew 132 people from 27 countries. Almost without exception, each participant was a practicing conservationist with a vital interest in the reasons for success or failure of projects reported by colleagues from other parts of the world.

The objectives of the workshop were threefold: (1) to compare experiences from successful soil and water conservation projects on steep lands as a means of determining the common principles involved that might be applied worldwide, (2) to publish the invited papers as a record of the magnitude of soil erosion worldwide and what accounts for the success or failure of efforts to deal with the erosion problem, and (3) to develop a manual useful to field technicians who must integrate soil and water conservation measures with improved agricultural production systems.

A book based on the workshop proceedings has been published by the Soil and Water Conservation Society. That book, *Conservation Farming on Steep Lands*, edited by myself and N. W. Hudson, is available from SWCS, 7515 Northeast Ankeny Road, Ankeny, Iowa 50021-9764, USA. It provides excellent background for anyone seeking real-life examples of the principles set forth in this manual.

Following the steeplands workshop, a group consisting of Jerome Arledge, Norman Hudson, Eric Roose, David Sanders, Francis Shaxson, Mohamed El-Ashry, Jerry Hammond, Max Schnepf, and myself stayed on in Puerto Rico for several days to work on this guidelines manual. It was agreed by this group that there are a great many specific instructions available for field technicians. What was needed more were guidelines of a much broader nature.

This manual should prove valuable to a broad spectrum of interests, from soil conservationists attempting to raise the awareness level of policymakers, to project leaders attempting to explain problems and solutions to their administrators or funding groups, to nonconservationists charged with establishing conservation measures while producing agronomic and tree crops.

During the steep lands workshop, it had become apparent that most workshop participants held the philosophy that production must be the primary objective of agriculture. While conservation is essential, especially on steep lands, it is a secondary and complementary objective that must be integrated with production practices. This is a departure from past thinking in which conservation often was the primary objective and sometimes the only objective. Also, workshop participants felt that mechanical erosion control should be used only if necessary for water control, where agronomic and agroforestry measures are insufficient. This guidelines manual very much reflects this philosophy.

Most of the credit for this manual must go to Francis Shaxson who wrote all of the early drafts and to Norman Hudson and David Sanders who spent considerable time and effort diligently reviewing each draft and making constructive suggestions.

W. C. Moldenhauer

Chapter 1

Introduction

S oil erosion threatens millions of hectares of land in developed and developing countries alike. In some locations the problem is getting worse. Rapidly rising populations push people onto steeper, more fragile land, which is then farmed more and more intensively.

Where steep slopes must be farmed for food, feed, or fiber production, soil erosion results in both on-site and off-site impacts. There are many cases where all of the productive soil has washed from fields or where expensive reservoirs have filled rapidly with sediment.

These erosion problems continue in spite of expensive control programs and interventions. Aid agency officials are increasingly self-critical of past programs, and environmental interests continue to emphasize sustainable development.

Professional conservationists and development advisors are suggesting new ways to approach erosion control, and new methodologies for planning development are emerging. These include the Diagnosis and Design Methodology derived for agroforestry by the International Council for Research in Agroforestry, the Farming Systems Research approach developed by the International Maize and Wheat Improvement Center, and the training approach developed by the Soil and Water Conservation and Land Utilization Program of the Southern African Development Coordination Conference, with the assistance of the Commonwealth Secretariat, described as Integrated Conservation Farming Systems.

Why Success or Failure?

In view of all of these developments, the World Association of Soil and Water Conservation and the Soil Conservation Society of America (now the Soil and Water Conservation Society) held a workshop in March 1987 in San Juan, Puerto Rico, where conservationists dealing with erosion problems on steep lands compared experiences, both successful and unsuccessful. One objective of the workshop was to determine common principles that could be applied over a broad spectrum of the world's cultivated steep lands.

Many interesting and important facts came to light during the workshop. There was a broad base of agreement among participants on how to achieve soil and water conservation on steep lands and why past efforts often failed. Perhaps the most recurring theme was that approaches of the past relied too heavily on structures that may have been expensive to build and maintain and that added little to the productivity of the land. In fact, the structures may have been disruptive to the objectives of individual farmers. With no enthusiasm for maintenance of these unwanted structures, they soon fell into disrepair and became ineffective in conserving either soil or water.

While recognizing the fact that the supplementary need for structural measures must not be forgotten or underrated, it is much more effective to develop a plan or strategy for increased production and efficiency with the farmer, using structural measures, if necessary, to complement an effective system of land husbandry. Better management of crops, pastures, forests, and soil retains more water for productive use by plants and for maintaining streamflow. Lowering raindrop splash and runoff reduces the amount of soil that is dislocated and transported away from where it is needed—around plant roots.

Farmers, like these (from top) in Equador, Kuwait, and Indonesia, are the ultimate decision makers about how they will manage their land. A new approach to land husbandry must harmonize the views of conservationists with those of farmers.

Three Basic Ideas

To achieve effective soil and water conservation through proper land husbandry, three basic ideas are important:

1. *Farmers:* It is imperative to identify, engage, develop, and encourage the enthusiasm of individual farmers and communities in plant production activities.

2. *Husbandry:* The more fragile and erosion-prone an area is, the more urgent it is to give attention to producing, improving, and maintaining dense and long-lasting soil cover with useful plants and their residues. It is also important to encourage optimum conditions of soil structure and organic activity that satisfy the needs for good plant growth and encourage sufficient infiltration of water. These conditions, once achieved, must be maintained by disturbing them as little and as infrequently as possible.

3. *Runoff:* If flowing runoff is unavoidable, arrange for its safe disposal without causing erosion damage. A number of innovative, effective examples were cited during the workshop to reduce runoff velocity and to encourage the progressive formation of steps that reduce land slope. This is slower than "one-shot" terracing, but it

allows more time for change in the farmer's attitude and thus improves the probability of effective land management. It also reduces the cost of terracing to a fraction of that using hand labor or large machinery.

On cropped land, a protective mulch of leaves, litter, and crop residues is undoubtedly the most effective biological means of minimizing soil and water losses.

Good farming practice coincides with good farming in this intensive mixed cropping of vegetables in Java. Crops are grown in rotation throughout the year, giving good cover, and the raised beds on slight gradient provide the right combination of water conservation and drainage.

A Perspective

While it appeared that a publication was justified to elaborate these principles, workshop participants pointed out that there were many manuals on soil and water conservation already available. This meant that this publication must be broad enough to apply worldwide but not so general as to be of little use. We decided that technicians must rely on manuals and other information specific to their country or region for necessary details on soil, climate, adapted crops, grasses and trees, effective conservation measures and practices, etc. This publication is meant to provide a framework into which site-specific technical details can be fitted.

Chapter 2

Planning the Best Use of Land Resources

The world has the capacity to feed and clothe its current population, and there is some evidence that a much larger population could be sustained. Even in Africa, the continent suffering most from food shortage, there is untapped potential. But this does not help those countries that face the problem of trying to meet increasing food, fuel, and fiber demands from diminishing land resources.

Most food-deficit countries are too poor to buy what they need, and the countries with food surplus may respond to emergency famine relief operations, but are unlikely to continue this on a permanent basis. Most food-deficit countries do not have the resources to lift their agriculture even to the United Nations Food and Agriculture Organization (FAO) scenario of medium-level inputs. Moreover, transport logistics rule out the possibility of making up the food deficit in Africa by shipping surplus commodities from Europe and North America. The same applies to countries on the same continent. Surplus production within Africa may be used to alleviate temporary shortages in other countries, but this does not provide a long-term solution.

Neither is the opening up of new land always a practical solution. The potential for developing new land is severely limited in many countries, including some of the largest food-deficit nations. Increase in production, therefore, must come largely through better use of the land already in production. If there is unused land, the constraints that have hindered development in the past, such as poor soil or low rainfall, are not going to go away.

The solution must come from making better and more productive use of the land already farmed. Many agricultural development programs have been disappointing, but there are also examples of substantial improvement in national production. Twenty years ago, India suffered frequent, serious famine. Now, the country is self-sufficient in cereal production in most years and exports some grain in good years. The sad record in Africa draws attention away from progress in other regions, particularly Southeast Asia.

One of the critical issues in agricultural development in the Third World is the risk of land degradation. Compared with more temperate, northern climates, the land in much of the Third World is more vulnerable to degradation, and the climate is more damaging. Consequently, trying to prevent soil degradation has been an important part of agricultural development programs, though the approaches used have not worked. In spite of expenditures on agricultural development in Africa, per capita production has gone down; in spite of soil conservation efforts, erosion is as severe as ever. However, from the experience and mistakes of the past, a new approach is emerging that offers a solution to better, wiser, and more productive use of the land.

Lessons from the Past

Huge amounts of money and human effort have gone into agricultural development and soil conservation programs during the last 20 or 30 years. The return on this investment has been poor, and the sad state of the situation worldwide has been dramatized by many writers and researchers. However, the world predicament is not entirely unrelieved gloom. Paul Harrison's *The Greening of Africa* tells stories that offer hope, rather like Kusum Nair's *Blossoms in the Dust,* which shows fragments of hope among the desperate poverty in India. Some believe and many hope the decline in Africa can be reversed by better management of the continent's resources.

The previous approach to agricultural development and soil conservation programs was mainly "top-down." It was customary to assume that conservationists or extensionists knew what was right and what was needed by farmers. If farmers were reluctant to accept the plan, the conservationists' or extensionists' response was to increase the "hard sell" to convince them, or to try to change their way of thinking. If necessary, the governments were prepared to pay for unpopular works to be constructed. And if all else failed, legislation might be used to force compliance among farmers.

In some cases, this approach slowed the rate of land degradation by putting on the ground a defense system of mechanical works. Examples from Africa are the grass strips in Swaziland, the contour banks in Lesotho, and the terracing in Ethiopia. But these and similar programs did little or nothing to improve production, even when the introduction of improved farming practices was supposed to be part of the package.

Such programs tried to attack erosion head-on, rather

than to tackle the real cause—poor land management. The programs were unpopular because they did not align with farmers' needs and wishes. There was little involvement by farmers and no subsequent maintenance. Faced with this lack of enthusiasm among farmers, soil conservation became unpopular with politicians and governments.

The new approach says that participation by the people is paramount, and better land management must be a bottom-up or grass-roots movement. The people must be involved at all stages—from the identification of program objectives to program implementation. If a program is popular among farmers, it will be picked up and supported by politicians as soon as the cause is seen to be a vote winner rather than a vote loser. Researchers and extensionists must start thinking of people as part of the solution, not as part of the problem.

The program must depend upon offering short-term benefits because the subsistence farmer cannot wait for long-term benefits. Also, the results must be things the farmer perceives as benefits. For the western commercial farmer, the prime objective is usually an increase in production or an increase in profitability. The subsistence farmer may have quite different objectives. An increase in the reliability of production, that is, an increase in food security, may be more important than yield; or perhaps

It is important to include farmers at all stages of planning for soil and water conservation on their land.

Farmers' decisions about land use are often strongly influenced by market conditions.

an objective is to achieve a better return per unit input of seed, fertilizer, or labor. To achieve the same production with less labor may be an objective, for labor is a critical constraint in many communities. The assumption that cheap labor is abundant in developing countries is not true in many situations.

Even in countries where subsistence agriculture predominates, there is usually some form of cash cropping, perhaps producing fruit, vegetables, or poultry for casual sales, or the sale of surplus staples in a year when the crop exceeds the domestic requirement. The growth of this agricultural sector depends upon the triple incentives of input availability, market outlets, and reasonable prices. In some countries, the deliberate holding down of farm prices for political reasons has seriously curtailed production. There are also cases where the incentive of a good price has led to dramatic increases in national production, for example, maize in Mexico in 1980 and maize in Zimbabwe in 1987.

The primary objective of land management should be improved, sustainable production through good land husbandry. Control of soil erosion control follows as a consequence. This is a reversal of the previous idea that it is necessary to conserve the soil in order to get better crops. The new message is this: aim to improve the soil conditions for root growth and crop production and, in so doing, achieve better conservation of water and soil.

Perhaps when the excellent FAO publication "Protect and Produce" is next reprinted, the sequence could be reversed and the title changed to "Produce and Protect."

Aid programs usually work through fixed-term projects, typically three to five years. But experience shows that long-term programs are necessary to achieve significant improvements in agricultural production. Programs need time for training and time to learn from experience and to make refinements. Where the budgeting system of aid or technical assistance organizations requires funding to be in short, fixed-term segments, the donors should, in the jargon of development economists, "buy a time-slice of the program." In other words, the donor supports one part of a long-term program worked out by the receiving country.

New Strategies

To increase agricultural production, every country should have a national strategy for the use and development of its natural resources. This strategy should include basic principles, for example, maximizing production from the best land and minimizing the use of marginal land. The plan should aim to match the use and management of land to its physical characteristics and capabilities. The object is for all parts of the land surface to remain as productive in the future as they are now, so management should be related to the danger of land "wearing out" (see page 25).

There may be conflicting interests to resolve in putting together a national agricultural development plan. For example, government is likely to seek increased production of export crops to help the nation's balance of payments, while farmers are likely to place more emphasis on food production and food security. A major purpose in developing a long-term national strategy is to arrive at an acceptable compromise between differing objectives.

In an important paper presented at a 1988 conference in Bangkok, David Sanders of FAO pointed out that "soil conservationists have, in the past, concentrated on *what* is happening, rather than *why* it is happening." Sanders urged that authorities be led to understand the real causes of the problem so they can direct their efforts toward the causes rather than the symptoms. "This may lead to the conclusion," he said, "that the problem cannot be overcome until some major change is made in, perhaps, the local marketing structure, the taxation systems, the land tenure laws, or in some other field in which the present-day soil conservationist does not usually become involved."

The starting point for a national strategy must be a baseline inventory of natural resources. The technique rapidly growing in popularity is the geographical information system (GIS). A GIS permits the computerized compilation of the type of data base that was formerly contained in a variety of different forms, such as geological surveys, soil surveys, and meteorological and hydrological records—data bases that are not easy to combine. Digitiz-

Where a soil's organic matter has been destroyed by burning or excessive grazing and soil structure collapses because of excessive cultivation, the land may lose all of its stability and productivity.

ing this information for computer storage not only improves storage and retrieval but allows the different sources of data to be combined with digitized topographic or remote sensing data.

This new GIS technique allows developing countries to build rapidly the kind of natural resource data base that once required decades of field surveys. The next step is to use the data to formulate a national strategy for how best to develop the available resources. Methods and techniques for doing this have also been developed and much improved in recent years.

The lack of political will is related to the unpopularity of earlier soil conservation strategies. What is required now is to change the product, not the marketing. If agricultural development results in an increase in the quality of life in rural areas, the policies and the politicians become more popular. This strengthens the rural element in politics and tends to redress the usual imbalance between the political power base of cities versus rural areas.

The concept of achieving soil conservation through good land husbandry means that soil conservation becomes an integral part of agriculture and extension. The effectiveness of a single, combined service for extension and soil conservation was demonstrated more than 30 years ago in Africa by CONEX, the Department of Conservation and Extension of the Federal Government of Rhodesia and Nyasaland (comprising what are now Zim-

In the end, farmers themselves must act, individually and collectively, if land husbandry is to be improved.

LAND HUSBANDRY

babwe, Zambia, and Malawi)—a model with many features still relevant today.

One problem today is that few developing countries have an effective extension service. Even in countries with strong government support and outside financial assistance, the sheer logistics of making contact with huge numbers of small-scale farmers are overwhelming. Trying to solve the problem through "T and V" (the Training-and-Visits System, sometimes cynically called the touch-and-vanish method) means dilution to the point where only the most simple messages can be transmitted. Extension services, like conservation services, need to change to working with farmers rather than telling farmers what to do.

Many different factors affect farmers' decisions about land use and management. Better land husbandry can only occur through spontaneous actions of various kinds on the part of farmers.

But decisions are often necessary by national and state governments to provide a suitable climate in terms of coherent and stable policies for extension strategies, for costs and prices, for incentives, for storage and marketing, and for other aspects. Given this improved climate, farmers can then make decisions that will result simultaneously in the satisfaction of their requirements and the stability and continued productivity of their land resources.

The adjustment of these wider issues involving government policies may be of overriding importance to the development of more productive, sustainable forms of land use. Without such adjustments, farmers may be pushed toward inappropriate systems of land use and management, whether they like them or not. These are important issues, but issues outside the scope of this text.

Tactics for Action

A common assumption in the past has been that security of tenure is necessary before farmers will invest in land improvement. This applied particularly when programs emphasized long-term developments, for example, building terraces with a long pay-back justification. Also, communal grazing rights may inhibit the adoption of controlled grazing as part of improved management. However, several examples were reported at the Puerto Rico workshop showing that good land husbandry can be achieved without freehold tenure. Security of access may be the important feature rather than security of tenure.

The new approach will try to minimize interventions that require external incentives or subsidies because the idea is that the program should be attractive to farmers without these props. However, there are some cases where external support may be justified, for example, activities that have a long time period before the benefits accrue, such as forestry, or activities that will benefit an entire community, such as gully control or reclamation on communal land. Where the main beneficiary is the state rather than the individual land user, it is reasonable that the state support the works.

The new philosophy puts more emphasis on management of rainfall and runoff, stressing water conservation more than soil conservation. Similarly, the main objective is maintaining and improving soil productivity instead of the earlier concern with reducing soil loss.

The design and planning of sustainable land use will continue to include some use of structures, such as terraces, drains, and channels. But where previously structures were seen as the starting point for improved land use, to be followed by improved agronomy, the new philosophy assumes that the primary thrust should be better soil management, with structures used only when they are unavoidable. Also, when structures are used, they should require minimum inputs both for initial construction and for maintenance.

Chapter 3

Principles of Land Husbandry

Effective action to prevent or to control soil erosion and water runoff is generally not an integral part of people's use and management of land. The seriousness of erosion and runoff problems is growing, and both affect the livelihood of an increasing number of small farmers struggling for subsistence. Both also diminish the profitability of other forms of rural land use, including forestry and animal production. Because most countries have little or no reserve of unused, good land, more marginal land, especially steep and semiarid areas, is being brought into cultivation.

If the methods of managing this land do not prevent its degradation, its use will not be sustainable. Other land will continue to be brought into production, if only to compensate for the loss of productivity on that land already cultivated.

Erosion and runoff also increase costs to urban communities. Damaged roads and bridges must be repaired, sandbanks and diminished streamflow during dry periods

If the methods of managing marginal land do not prevent its degradation, its use will not be sustainable.

Severe soil erosion reduces crop production by exposing plant roots and limiting plant uptake of nutrients and water.

impede river navigation, river water needs additional treatment for domestic and other uses, agricultural production outputs decline on eroded land, and the effects of floods must be countered.

Soil conservation practices are often advocated to farmers as necessary for increased plant production in the future. Such practices are often also urged upon farmers because of additional benefits to the community or the state. But even though it is the farmers who are supposed to benefit, they often give these recommendations only lukewarm reception.

Why don't farmers readily adopt soil conservation recommendations? Some explanations include the following:

► Producing plants—crops, pasture grasses, and trees—from the land is the chief aim of farmers. However, soil conservation generally is promoted as an end in itself and as a collection of actions to be added on to normal land use activities.

► Farmers are only likely to adopt recommendations if they increase income, reduce risk, reduce the drudgery of farming, or increase social standing in the community. The recommended soil conservation practices in many cases do not offer these benefits.

► Long-term benefits are usually offered as the justification for soil conservation actions. The time horizon for these long-term benefits is beyond that of farmers, who see little hope of improving their present situation by adopting the recommendations.

► In many situations, especially where heavy reliance is placed on physical works to solve erosion problems, imported technology turns out to be inappropriate, and farmers perceive no significant benefits.

► Programs aimed at conserving soil often are planned and executed without regard to farmers' views, aims, wishes, or preferences. Because they have not been involved in the planning of the works and because they have not considered the works to be particularly useful, farmers feel little obligation to maintain them, which often results in failure of the programs.

The aims of farmers and conservationists thus do not always coincide, and farmers often feel that the recommendations are irrelevant to their situation.

A Different Approach

Given this unsatisfactory situation, it is unlikely that merely repeating the current message more forcefully, in more detail, or to a wider audience is going to provoke much improvement. A new approach must (1) encourage the intensification of plant production from land without provoking soil destruction, (2) integrate conservation into agricultural practices, and (3) harmonize the views of conservationists with those of farmers.

A rearrangement of current knowledge and experience brings new insights, which offer new possibilities for solving problems of land degradation and suggest the following changes in emphasis or mental "switches":

Farmers are interested in improving the yields of the plants they grow. Management practices designed to increase photosynthetic leaf area—to a level consistent with producing required levels of yield—and the development of root systems also favor the protection of the soil surface, infiltration of rainwater, reduction of runoff, and may improve the regularity of streamflow. Thus, actions to im-

Tobacco provides virtually no soil protection from rain after harvest. In this Kasungu, Malawi, tobacco field (top), the darker clay and organic soil fractions have eroded away, leaving the sandier fractions behind. On steeper slopes (bottom), even the sandy fractions eroded away.

prove yields can also be means of achieving conservation of water and soil.

Erosion and runoff are not primary causes of land degradation, but foreseeable ecological consequences of inappropriate land use and management. They are usually only symptoms of other problems that may affect plant growth directly. Attention should, therefore, focus on helping farmers to improve their management of the land as a means of furthering their own goals, and in so doing keep soil and water in place.

Intense rainfall can damage unprotected soil by splash and by surface sealing. Reducing these damaging effects of rainfall should be a primary concern. Cover on and over the soil provides the needed protection. Physical conservation works cannot diminish the effects of rainfall; they are designed only to reduce erosion damage by runoff. Actions that reduce the effects of raindrop impact will also reduce selective removal of the more fertile soil fractions, maintain infiltration, minimize runoff, and prevent the smoothing of rough soil surfaces.

Plant yields are reduced more by a shortage or excess of soil moisture than they are by loss of soil. If rainfall, soil moisture, and runoff are managed well, plant growth can be maximized and the soil will remain in place.

A number of soil conservation practices currently recommended will be more readily understood by farmers if the benefits of these practices are pointed out in terms of better water management and plant production. These practices include improvements in organic matter, soil structure, and crop cover; crop rotations; proper use of fertilizers; contour planting; bench terracing; and other manipulations of the land surface.

The worth of practices recommended to increase production must be evaluated both in terms of their potential to increase yields and in terms of their conservation effectiveness. Each measure of value should be used.

Farmers are manipulating agroecosystems that are continually adjusting and being adjusted in response to climatic variation and to social and economic pressures. Static soil conservation measures, such as physical structures, can only be fully effective when they are used as complements to, and not substitutes for, good management that combines maintenance of high yields and effective conservation.

Most soils have an inherent capacity for recuperation after they have become degraded as an environment for root growth and, hence, for plant production. This capacity depends more upon biological processes in the upper layers of the soil than upon weathering processes at the bottom of the soil profile. Emphasis should be given to increasing the quantity of organic materials and organic processes in the soil to safeguard and strengthen this capacity.

Increasing evidence from many parts of the world

Raindrops erode bare soil not protected by crop leaves. The more cover, the better the protection from soil loss in this Namadzi, Malawi, tobacco field.

suggests that approaches can be made more acceptable and more effective in the future by emphasizing these six points:

1. Soil conservation should be an integral part of any farming system rather than a separate discipline or activity.

2. Loss of soil productivity is more important than the amount of soil loss.

3. Rainwater management is more important than soil conservation.

4. Biological measures are more significant than mechanical measures in preventing erosion and runoff.

5. Reduction of runoff should precede attempts to control its flow.

6. Action programs based on bottom-up cooperation between technical staff and local communities are far more likely to succeed and last than those based on top-down planning.

Where soil cannot absorb rainwater fast enough, large volumes of runoff may be generated, even on relatively flat land, which is the case on this Vertisol near Indore, India.

Conservation and Husbandry

Conservation is a concept that has been broadly defined as "prolonging the useful life of resources." Unless there is a commitment by people to look after their natural resources, not only for themselves but for future generations as well, the concept becomes meaningless.

Applied to land, the objective of conservation is to work out how to satisfy people's aesthetic and physical needs from the land without harming or destroying its capacity to go on satisfying those needs in the future. R. G. Downes described soil conservation as "the positive task of devising and implementing systems of land use and management so that there shall be no loss of stability, productivity, or usefulness for the chosen purpose."

The concept of husbandry is widely understood when applied to crops and animals. As a concept signifying active understanding, management, and improvement, it is equally applicable to land.

Crop husbandry, animal husbandry, and land husbandry all imply the following:

1. Understanding the characteristics, potentials, and limitations of different types of plants, animals, and land.

2. Predicting the likely positive or negative effects on their productivity resulting from a given change in management, or of severe but rare events, such as disease or severe rainfall.

3. Working out how they can be strengthened to resist the negative effects of such events.

4. Adopting systems of management that maintain their productivity and usefulness.

5. Improving their productivity in terms of quality and quantity of output in a given time.

6. The active and central role of the farmer as steward of the land.

Land and Land Use

Land is a complex and dynamic combination of factors—geology, topography, hydrology, soils, microclimates, and communities of plants and animals—that are continually interacting under the influence of climate and of people's activities. These interactions are continuously taking place and will continue to do so regardless of how clearly they are perceived or understood.

Land varies from place to place because of past differences in these interactions. These variations in land must be identified and characterized if people are to understand the differing capabilities for various forms of use and the hazards of accelerated change and degradation that could accompany those uses. After forecasting how the land in a given place is likely to react to a change in its use, there exists the opportunity to define the most suitable form of management that will maintain the land's productivity and usefulness.

Changes in land use always bring about alterations in the relations among climate, soils, vegetation, topography, and water—alterations that represent adjustments in the system. Human interventions can upset less stable systems and start new cycles of erosion and change until different balances are reestablished. Increased surface runoff and erosion are two of the indications that such adjustments are occurring.

The three most frequent, negative effects of the agricultural modification of natural ecosystems, particularly where annual plants replace perennial plants, are as follows:

1. Degradation of the soil as a rooting environment.

2. Reduction in the number of species in the systems, thus reducing the systems' stability in the face of, for example, pests, diseases, or severe climatic events.

3. Alteration of the hydrologic cycle. Because soil surface layers may become less permeable, less rainfall soaks into the soil and a greater proportion becomes surface runoff. Excess water also may appear in the system because there is less transpiration than before.

Land is used in many ways to satisfy people's needs—to provide food, fiber, timber, and water; as sites for cities, industries, transport corridors, and recreation facilities; for mineral extraction and disposal of polluting wastes; for scientific study; and as reserves of space and of genetic materials for future use.

Land degradation is not solely an agricultural problem. It can be provoked by any of these uses if they are

This H-flume measures runoff from an area of cultivated Vertisols.

not appropriately planned, installed, and managed.

Arable agriculture is so different from natural systems that land degradation, principally in the form of erosion, salinization, and damage to soil structure, is more likely to occur under this use than under other imposed uses.

If agricultural systems are to be sustainable, they must be planned and managed using techniques and periods for soil recuperation. In this way it is possible to neutralize the soil-degrading effects of cultivation and of increased amounts of water in the system. Diversification and mixtures of crop enterprises for profit and for food security encourage the use of crop rotations, a powerful means of promoting soil recuperation on a regular basis.

Good land use is achieved when each required use has been located on suitable land and when each combination of land type and use is being managed in a way that avoids any degradation that might prevent such uses from being sustained.

Increasing demand for land for various uses generates fierce competition among users. The logical way to accommodate these needs is for governments to evaluate the land resources available, assess present and future requirements, and then allocate uses within areas to provide the optimum match between the land's ecological characteristics and the various uses imposed.

Soil Erosion and Landscape Stability

An important objective of land husbandry is for all parts of the land surface to remain at least as productive and as useful in the future as they are at present. No one unit of land should be allowed to "wear out" more quickly than any other unit.

But different land units subjected to the same inadequate management and to the same erosive rainfall will wear out at different rates. This is because of differences in soil depth, physical characteristics, slope, fertility, and drainage.

The more often erosive splash and runoff occur on a given soil, the greater will be the rate of productivity decline.

A given depth of soil lost by erosion over a given time from a deep soil represents a slower rate of loss in its total "store" of productivity than the same depth of soil lost over the same period from a shallow soil.

Similarly, if the same rate of soil loss by erosion occurs on a soil with even distribution of fertility throughout the profile as on another soil where all the fertility is concentrated in the upper layers, the rate of productivity loss will be proportionately slower in the former than

Shallow soils (top) will lose productive capacity more quickly than deep soils (bottom) if subjected to the same rates of erosion from the surface.

in the latter Figures 1a and 1b).

The productive potential in the upper layers of any soil will remain unimpaired by erosion if the rate of formation in the A-horizon balances with the rate of erosion from the surface. However, the rate of surface soil loss under most agricultural conditions is usually greater than the rate of soil formation by deep weathering at the bottom of the profile. Therefore, even when erosion loss is balanced by A-horizon formation, there will usually be a reduction in depth over the years (Figure 2a).

Where erosion loss from the soil surface is greater than the rate of A-horizon formation, the reduction in depth will be more rapid, accompanied by the loss of topsoil and the exposure of subsoil layers, perhaps even bedrock (Figure 2b).

Soil depth will only remain constant when the average rate of loss from the soil surface is no greater than the rate of subsoil development from parent material. Encouragement of biological activity in the A-horizon promotes the formation of humic materials from organic substrates, all of which contributes to better soil structure. Improved structure diminishes soil erodibility and favors plant root growth. An appropriate combination of good structure and adequate cover can limit surface erosion

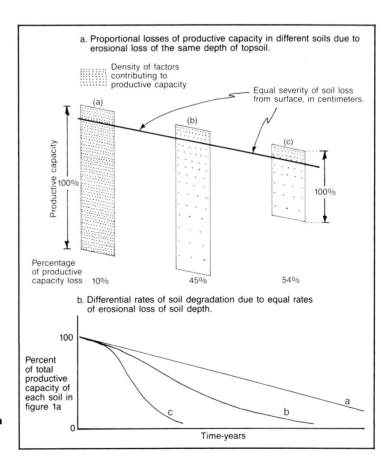

a. Proportional losses of productive capacity in different soils due to erosional loss of the same depth of topsoil.

Density of factors contributing to productive capacity

Equal severity of soil loss from surface, in centimeters.

Productive capacity

100%

100%

Percentage of productive capacity loss   10%   45%   54%

b. Differential rates of soil degradation due to equal rates of erosional loss of soil depth.

100

Percent of total productive capacity of each soil in figure 1a

0

Time-years

Figure 1. Differential rates of loss in productive capacity on different soils suffering the same rate of loss in depth.

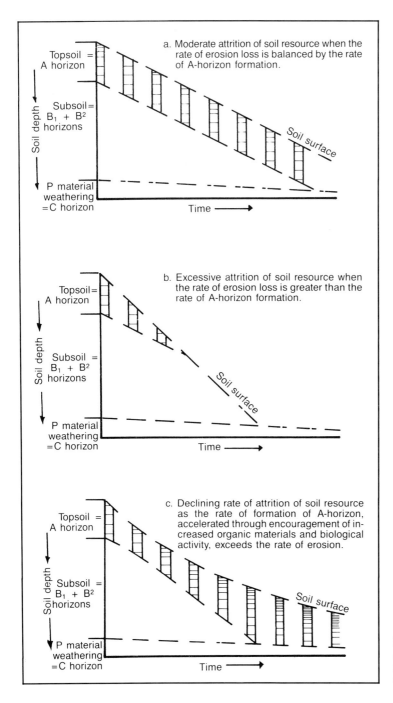

Figure 2. Significance of A-horizon management in maintaining soil productive capacity.

losses to insignificant levels. Under suitable management, the A-horizon may be deepened both by accumulation of plant residues at the top and by extending the depth of modification of subsoil materials at the bottom (Figure 2c).

Greater care and more rapid improvements in management are needed in shallow soils, in soils where fertility is concentrated in the upper layers, in soils with low rates of soil formation downward from the surface (A-horizon formation) and upward from the parent material (deep weathering), and in soils on steep slopes that favor

Excessive grazing compacts the soil surface and exposes it to raindrop impact. Although erosion may not be severe, much of the incident rainfall may run off.

rilling, gullying, or mass-movement. Any action is beneficial that encourages plant growth with associated protection of the soil surface; encourages biological regeneration of good physical conditions, particularly in the upper soil horizons; minimizes damage to desirable soil structural conditions; and improves rainfall infiltration.

Soil conservation cannot work miracles by instantly returning degraded land to a state of full and sustainable productivity. Physical works cannot make up for the effects of poor land use and management.

The first and most important step in achieving conservation of soil and water is to ensure that the use and management of the land in any particular area is appropriate to the characteristics of that land.

Matching Land Uses to Land Types

The most appropriate way to match land uses to land types is to locate those uses that provide the most protection on the most hazardous areas of land and to use the least hazardous areas for those uses that offer the least protection.

Land varies in its ability to provide suitable environmental conditions for different uses. It also varies in its stability and its capacity to resist erosive forces when subjected to inadequate management. Land suitability classification characterizes the former, and land capability classification the latter.

Land capability classification permits the ranking of the land's natural units according to their relative erosion hazards. Combining this information with the distribution and characteristics of different soils across an area enables the delineation of distinct units of land that differ according to their management needs.

Within the boundary of any one such unit, a specific form of management for the chosen use is applied to give even crop yields over the entire unit. In a neighboring unit, different management may be needed to achieve the same or similar result.

Different forms of land use vary in their capacity to protect or damage land resources. It is not sufficient to classify the many different types of agricultural use into "annual crops," "pastures," or "forests." This is because the ways in which they are managed have significant effects on their capacity for production and on their protective characteristics. These are closely related to the amount of low-level cover that they provide to the soil surface and to the ways in which their management affects soil structural conditions. For example, poorly managed pasture on a steep slope with compacted soils and little vegetative cover may be a less productive or protective use than a well-managed system of annual crops under minimum tillage and maintenance of excellent cover and structural conditions on the same slope.

Perennial crops, such as citrus, coconut, and apple trees, provide almost no effective protection to any bare soil beneath them. They may be too widely spaced to provide an even cover on the one hand, and on the other the leaves are so far off the ground that big water drops gain high speed before reaching the soil surface. It is the low-growing grasses, legumes, or mulch covering the soil surface between the trees of a well-managed plantation that provide protection, not the trees themselves.

If uniform management is applied equally across an area, which is in fact a mosaic of units of differing char-

Inappropriate matching of land use to land type on this Peruvian hillslope led to severe erosion and subsequent abandonment of the land for cropping purposes.

A wide-spaced perennial crop (apple trees) with a good, low ground cover on conservation banks represents an appropriate match of land use to land type.

acteristics, that management will be appropriate for some of the area and less appropriate for the remainder. By affecting crop cover and yields to different extents, this may unnecessarily expose parts of the area to risk of degradation; it may also represent an inefficient use of inputs.

In many situations, current land use may appear inappropriately matched with land type, such as the poorly managed cultivation of annual crops on steep slopes normally considered nonarable in an area of erosive rainfall. Often, for social or political reasons, a change in land use, from annual cropping to forest plantations, for example, may be impossible. Nevertheless, a better matching of use with land type can often be made by improving the characteristics of the current use. For example, improvements in the physical and chemical conditions of fertility can enhance crop yields, with which are associated a better cover of plant leaves and litter above and on the soil surface.

The better the characteristics of the use are matched with the characteristics of the land, the easier it will be to keep that use productive and the land stable.

Farmers' Viewpoints and Motivations

Farmers, not planners, are the people who decide what will and will not be done on agricultural land. They make rational decisions according to their own circumstances. What they decide will be influenced by physical factors, such as soil and climate; the technical advice and assistance available to them; the socioeconomic features of the community; and their own personal situation.

Land use decisions by farmers can be strongly influenced by nonagricultural factors—social, economic, and political—and these factors may be more important than the technical considerations discussed in these guidelines. For instance, the "correct" planting date for a crop may be determined more by recommendations from a local astrologer, based on the positions of the stars, than by those of the agricultural extensionist, based on soil moisture conditions; insecurity of land tenure may inhibit farmers from investing in permanent improvements to the land; changes in the prices of inputs will affect the amounts used; changes in a government's agricultural policy may affect the incentives or disincentives that influence the farmer's choice of crop.

Such factors are usually beyond the capability of the farmer or extensionist to change, but they can set the boundaries within which any improvement in land use and management must be decided, designed, and implemented.

In the past, farmers who did not accept or implement technical recommendations were said to be uncooperative, stubborn, and unreasonable. Advancement was sought by attempting to change the farmers' rationality. But farmers with few resources are artists in survival. Their reasoning is effective in reaching what they see as objectives, within their own limitations. It is more likely that outside constraints and pressures require changing before farmers' rational decision-making can produce better results (Figure 3).

In this context, an unwillingness to adopt conservation practices that do not appear to do the job or to provide any perceptible short-term benefits appears entirely reasonable. It thus makes sense to approach soil conservation indirectly, primarily by helping farmers to do better what they prefer doing—producing plants—in the knowledge that better conservation of resources will be an automatic consequence of their actions.

A farmer's problems can be approached with a wider viewpoint than purely soil conservation. For instance:

1. Are crop yields low? Is the problem really one of poor soil structure rather than of soil erosion?

2. Is it difficult to cultivate the field because of so many stones? Why not collect them into lines along the

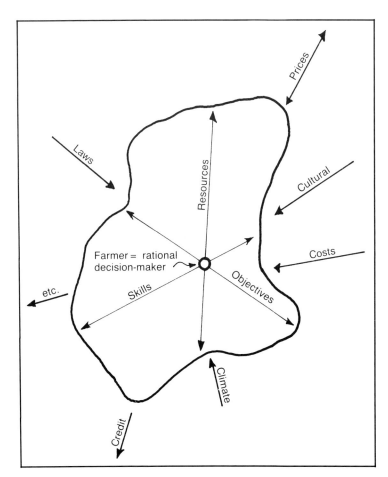

Figure 3. A farmer makes rational decisions within an "envelope" of constraints and potentials.

contour as a way of getting them out of the way—and forming the basis of some terraces?

3. Do cattle need more fodder? What about using roadside banks and terrace lines or streambanks to plant useful fodder grasses—and to provide some stable protection for the bare soil?

4. Is more firewood or timber needed on the farm? Terrace lines or streambanks again could be put to good use by planting trees along them—also helping to strengthen the banks.

There are instances where traditional practices can effectively conserve soil and water. In the past, such practices often were overlooked by technical advisers. Field experience shows that farmers may welcome and adopt improvements to these known and familiar practices, already integrated into present farming systems, much more readily than they will adopt alien recommendations that they feel do not fit their needs.

A farmer who successfully adopts advice for improvements in what he is already doing gains confidence in his own ability to initiate change and in his advisers. Improvements in his crops provide benefits in the short term and build on what he knows rather than expecting him to adopt new, untried practices that may involve unacceptable levels of risk or higher costs.

With growing confidence and a record of better crop yields, the farmer then becomes more open to suggestions for more radical changes and improvements that he would not earlier have accepted. Such recommendations might include some physical works if they are needed,

This Brazilian wheat crop shows the effects of soil compaction and limited water infiltration on production.

LAND HUSBANDRY

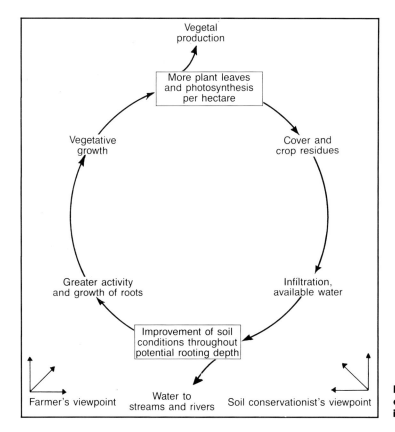

Figure 4. Farmers and soil conservationists: common interests, different viewpoints.

though the need for them will have been reduced by the effects of improved husbandry practices.

Farmers and soil conservationists in fact have several interests in common, although each group looks at these interests from different perspectives. A farmer's objective of better plant growth will be achieved through improvement of soil conditions in the profile, leading to greater activity and growth of roots, in turn leading to more vegetative growth with more leaves and photosynthesis. Simultaneously, this achieves the soil conservationist's objectives of more cover and crop residues, leading to more infiltration and available water, with less flood runoff and improved streamflow (Figure 4).

Conservation versus Reclamation

In the past, soil conservation was not always distinguished from land reclamation. Conservation implies continued good management of preferred land uses. Reclamation of severely degraded land implies drastic, costly action, usually including remedial changes in land use, soil amelioration, and construction of specialized works. All too often physical soil conservation practices were applied where they had no chance of success on their own because of the land's advanced state of degradation.

Inadequate husbandry has devastated this land in Kondoa, Tanzania.

As long as runoff was considered the chief cause of the erosion problem, conservation actions were often deemed unnecessary until the consequences of erosion were clearly visible, such as gullies and exposed subsoils. In response, physical works would be installed to control runoff. However, much effort and money was wasted, partly because the land had little remaining productive potential to be reclaimed and partly because such works were ineffective without changes in land use and management that addressed the true causes of the problem.

With this record, it is little wonder that economists, administrators, and politicians often consider soil conservation activities to be uneconomic and of low priority.

Because land husbandry aims to improve plant production and soil protection at the same time, thus achieving conservation of soil, the additional costs of conservation are generally low and to a large extent can be included in the costs of production. The increased production is also more likely to produce the cash that might be needed for any complementary physical conservation works.

Land husbandry techniques that ensure prevention of damage to the land should, therefore, be applied in every situation, but reclamation of seriously degraded land should only be attempted when there are compelling reasons to do so.

Chapter 4

Practicing the Principles on Sloping Lands

Good farming is good conservation. The better the condition of the soil for root growth and moisture storage, the better farmers' crops, trees, and pastures will grow. There will also be fewer and smaller runoff events, thus less transport of soil detached by rain splash or runoff.

A Sequential Look at Land Husbandry

Following is a sequence for looking at land husbandry:

Manage Rainfall, then Runoff. The two main processes of water erosion are detachment of soil by raindrop splash and transportation by surface runoff.

The two primary elements of control are, therefore, the maintenance of cover, which reduces soil splash, and the maximizing of infiltration, which reduces the volume and, hence, the velocity of surface runoff. Where runoff is unavoidable, additional control measures will be needed.

Where practical and desirable, encourage as much surface retention storage as possible. This will give water time to soak into the soil after rainfall has ended.

Minimize the erosive energy of unavoidable runoff by keeping it dispersed, shallow, and slow-flowing. This limits its potential for damage as it flows downhill. Uncontrolled runoff is water that might otherwise be put to good use.

Improve Soil Cover. Raindrops compact and seal the top few millimeters of the soil surface, particularly when the drops are large and their kinetic energy is greater. Cover over the soil dissipates the erosive energy of raindrops by breaking them up into smaller droplets whose energy is insufficient to splash soil particles or to compact the soil surface. If soil is not covered, the most valuable particles—clays and organic materials—are moved

Plant leaves break large, erosive raindrops into smaller droplets, which greatly reduces the erosive energy.

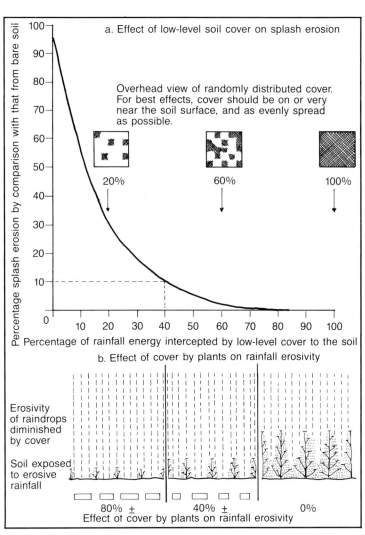

a. Effect of low-level soil cover on splash erosion

Overhead view of randomly distributed cover. For best effects, cover should be on or very near the soil surface, and as evenly spread as possible.

20%   60%   100%

Percentage splash erosion by comparison with that from bare soil

Percentage of rainfall energy intercepted by low-level cover to the soil

b. Effect of cover by plants on rainfall erosivity

Erosivity of raindrops diminished by cover

Soil exposed to erosive rainfall

80% ±   40% ±   0%

Effect of cover by plants on rainfall erosivity

Figure 5. Effects of low-level cover in reducing splash erosion and rainfall erosivity.

The same plant species can provide a varying amount of cover. Management is often more important than the plant species in determining how effectively vegetation intercepts rainfall.

36

further by splash and runoff than other soil materials, and the soil that remains behind is, therefore, impoverished.

Where about 40 percent of the soil's surface is protected by low-level (not more than one meter above the surface) and evenly distributed cover, splash erosion by raindrops may be reduced as much as 90 percent (Figure 5).

The leaf canopy of well-grown crops can provide effective soil cover while the crops are growing. The faster vegetative cover develops, the quicker will bare soil patches be protected, resulting in a smaller proportion of the season's total rainfall having erosive effects. A farmer's management decisions and skills influence this effect (Figure 6).

Crop residues left after harvest, or well-managed pastures or forests, also provide benefits to the soil and to subsequent crops because they protect the soil against rainfall impact. If runoff should occur, the residues help to slow its velocity. Residues also provide a source of organic materials that benefit root growth and soil structure. These materials have positive effects on the self-recuperating capacity of the soil (the build-up or restoration of soil structural units and their resistance to erosion by raindrop splash and surface flow), internal aeration and drainage of the soil, long-term availability of plant nutrients, and storage of soil moisture.

Any actions that diminish raindrop splash will directly or indirectly mitigate other aspects of the erosion process. Factors that favor infiltration and absorption of rainwater also favor root growth by increasing the amount of readily available soil moisture and prolonging the period over which plants can use it. These same factors can also extend the duration of flow in streams and rivers and minimize the frequency of flooding.

The soil surface is continually protected when a new crop is directly drilled through the residue of the previous crop.

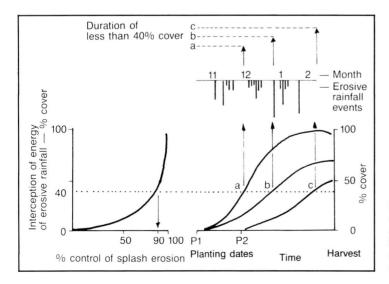

Figure 6. The development of crop cover, giving protection against erosive storms, can be accelerated by good management (a and b) or by early planting (b and c).

Improve Soil Structure and Rooting Conditions.

Surface soil can be pulverized and compacted by the frequent passage of animals or heavy machinery as well as by frequent or severe tillage. Pulverized soil is highly erodible and has a low infiltration rate; compacted soil also has a lower permeability.

Repeated cultivations to the same depth may cause a "pan" or layer of induced compaction at the bottom of the tilled layer. The "plow pan" resulting from repeated plowing with tractor- or ox-drawn equipment is best known, but repeated hand cultivation with a hoe can produce the same effect. Such a pan usually results in a low percolation rate, and its increased density may limit the volume of soil available for root growth and the storage of soil moisture.

Some soils have naturally occurring layers of densely packed materials, such as laterite or calcrete, which have the same effects as pans caused by cultivations. Aeration in compacted soils is reduced, and much of the soil moisture is held at tensions that make it unavailable to plant roots. Soil penetration by roots may be physically obstructed (Figure 7).

Where the infiltration rate is less than the rate of rainfall, excess water begins to accumulate on the surface as potential runoff as soon as surface layers of soil have become saturated.

Sealing and compaction of unprotected soil surfaces by large raindrops can occur in a few minutes. Damage by animal or vehicular traffic may take only a few seasons to develop. Pans below the tillage layer may become serious after a number of years. Naturally occurring pans take centuries or milennia to form. In badly managed soils, the first three types of damage may all occur simultaneously (Figure 8).

Catch Rain Where it Falls.

Plant roots tend to spread more or less evenly through the upper layers of soil. Water from rainfall should, therefore, also infiltrate as evenly as possible across the soil surface. It is important to catch and encourage infiltration of rainwater where and when it falls.

A farmer can help to maintain infiltration capacity with good soil structure and by keeping the soil surface rough with appropriate tillage or ridging. This strategy also minimizes the volume and velocity of potential runoff.

Increase Soil Moisture.

Roots require freely available soil moisture if they are to grow. The longer moisture is available, the less frequently plants will suffer moisture stress. The greater the depth to which soil moisture and air are freely available to plants, the greater the volume

An extremely sandy soil immediately after cultivation for the first crop following native vegetation and an adjacent plot after cultivation for the second crop. The soil is almost structureless and not resistant to erosion.

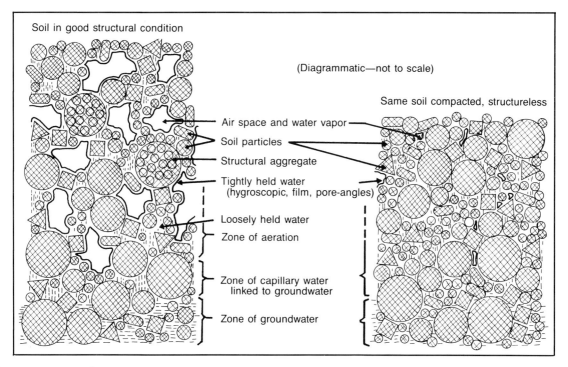

Soil in good structural condition

(Diagrammatic—not to scale)

Same soil compacted, structureless

Air space and water vapor

Soil particles

Structural aggregate

Tightly held water
(hygroscopic, film, pore-angles)

Loosely held water

Zone of aeration

Zone of capillary water
linked to groundwater

Zone of groundwater

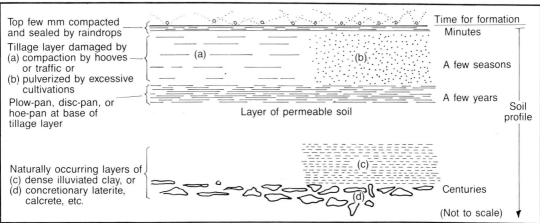

Top few mm compacted
and sealed by raindrops

Tillage layer damaged by
(a) compaction by hooves
    or traffic or
(b) pulverized by excessive
    cultivations

Plow-pan, disc-pan, or
hoe-pan at base of
tillage layer

Naturally occurring layers of
(c) dense illuviated clay, or
(d) concretionary laterite,
    calcrete, etc.

Time for formation

Minutes

(a)   (b)

A few seasons

A few years

Soil
profile

Layer of permeable soil

(c)

(d)   Centuries

(Not to scale)

Figure 7 (top). Compaction effects on soil structural conditions.

Figure 8 (bottom). Soil characteristics that reduce permeability and hinder root growth (not to scale).

of soil that can be explored by plant roots and the less often a lack of available soil moisture will become a limiting factor for plant development.

Where yield benefits are claimed from soil conservation practices, these benefits usually are more closely associated with water conservation and improvement in soil moisture availability than with any savings in soil and plant nutrients. Where soil conservation works really act as water conservation works, there may be more simple, less expensive, or more acceptable ways of achieving water savings. For instance, not burning crop residues increases protection of the soil surface and facilitates infiltration; not burning may even be more effective than building banks. Growing crops on a contoured ridge-and-furrow system may be more appropriate than bench terracing.

Increase Organic Activity in Soils. Organic materials and processes are of great importance in the formation, improvement, and maintenance of soil structure, which is essential for providing optimum conditions for root growth.

Rotational agriculture and mixed cropping, when well-planned and properly managed, restore organic materials and promote organic activity in one period of a rotation that may have declined during an earlier period of the rotation.

Rainfall, Runoff, and Streamflow in Small Catchments

The responses of streamflow to rainfall are more rapid and less complex in small catchments (tens or hundreds of hectares) than in large catchments (thousands of hectares). A change from undisturbed vegetation to agricultural land use generally leads to reduced cover and loss of soil structure. In almost all cases, these changes will produce more frequent runoff and higher peak flows.

The frequency and amount of runoff depends upon the infiltration rate, the volume of water already stored in the soil profile, and the frequency, duration, and intensity of storms. High volumes of runoff can follow both from storms of high intensity but short duration as well as from storms of low intensity but long duration. Severe storms generally occur infrequently, while less severe storms occur more often (Table 1).

In a small catchment, changes in land use—whether causing degradation or improvement—made by relatively small numbers of people may nevertheless affect a significant proportion of the land surface and thus have a marked effect on infiltration, runoff, and streamflow. In a big catchment, changes in land use over small areas have little effect on overall streamflow; only drastic changes over large portions of the catchment will cause significant changes in the relation between rainfall and the expected pattern of riverflow.

Table 1. The volume of rainfall that becomes runoff depends upon the severity of a rainstorm and upon soil conditions.

Condition of Soil— Infiltration, Percolation, Soil-Moisture Storage	Frequency and Severity of Expected Maximum Rainstorm		
	On Average Once in 10 Years	On Average Once in 5 Years	On Average Once Every Year
	Very Severe	Severe	Moderate
	Expected volume of runoff will be		
Excellent	Moderate	Small	Very Small
Moderate	Large	Moderate	Small
Poor	Very large	Large	Moderate

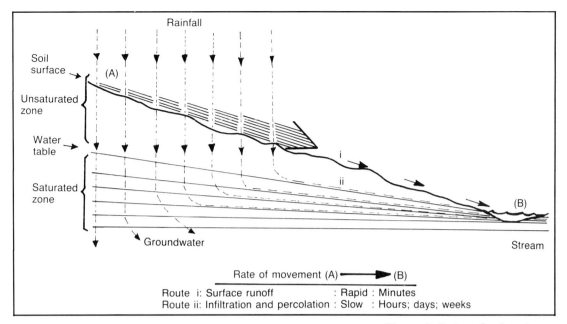

Route i: Surface runoff : Rapid : Minutes
Route ii: Infiltration and percolation : Slow : Hours; days; weeks

Figure 9. Rates of rainwater movement to a stream by surface and subsurface routes.

In arid and semiarid areas, rainstorms are often intense, runoff may be rapid, evaporation rates are high, and little rainfall may penetrate far into the soil or accumulate as a water table capable of sustaining streamflow. Consequently, streams from small catchments in these areas are often ephemeral, flowing only during storms and for a short time thereafter.

Rainwater that has infiltrated the soil surface and percolated below the root zone to a water table moves slowly, perhaps taking as much as six months to move from where it entered the soil to the streambank where it may reappear. On the other hand, rainwater that does not enter the soil but moves as surface runoff will travel the same distance much more quickly, in a matter of minutes or hours (Figure 9).

In most places, rainstorms are more or less intermittent. When rainwater can easily enter the soil and move downward through the profile, soil moisture reserves in the root zone will be replenished more quickly and additional water will move sooner below the root zone toward any underlying water table (Figure 10).

In small catchments where a high proportion of rainfall becomes surface runoff, a stream will flood more often and to greater heights than where most rainfall infiltrates into the soil. Practices that minimize surface runoff also minimize flooding severity downstream.

In a small catchment where land management is deteriorating, the water table may not be replenished adequately by infiltrated rainwater each year. During dry weather, there may be insufficient groundwater left to feed the stream, which may then cease to flow earlier each year, thus remaining dry for longer periods.

In catchments where larger volumes of rainfall have infiltrated, flow in streams and rivers will be prolonged into or even throughout the dry season. However, the total annual volume in the river may be less than in a poorly vegetated catchment because of increased loss to the atmosphere by transpiration through deep-rooted plants.

The advantages of less flood damage and more regular streamflow in improved agricultural catchments generally outweigh any disadvantages because of lower total annual streamflow.

Action in Catchments

Topographic catchments, which are the units of land that collect rainfall and runoff, are the logical landscape units on which to organize land use—from agriculture to urban development. The topographic crests around a watercourse make the enclosed catchment an independent unit of land with respect to surface hydrology. What happens on the catchment slopes affects both the quality and regularity of streamflow.

However, it may not always be possible to implement improved conservation of water and soil over an entire catchment. Some landholders may be unable or unwilling to take part in the process, especially if, as so often was the case in the past, the plan relies on layouts of physical conservation works across whole catchment surfaces. Even where emphasis is placed on better management of land to raise yields, many farmers in a catchment may not join the movement in its initial stages, often waiting to see what benefits are achieved by the more adventurous initiators. In such a situation, it is more appropriate to begin working with willing groups of neighboring farmers than to

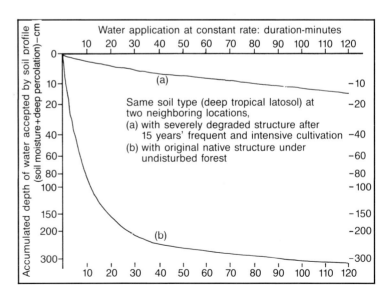

Figure 10. Rates of soil moisture recharge and deep percolation under two different management regimes.

A river near Umuarama, Brazil, showing signs of instability in the catchment. The wide, sandy deposits indicate sediment-laden floods occur alternately with low water flows.

start with individual farms scattered across the landscape. There are several reasons for this:

1. Neighbors who are willing to work together on common problems of land use can provide each other with mutual support and encouragement in making new decisions and adopting improved practices.

2. The benefits of improved water infiltration over several farms can have a perceptible effect on the streamflow from the subcatchments dominated by the group of farms.

3. It is likely that neighbors can agree on an overall layout across their farms of any physical measures that might be needed, such as conservation banks and waterways for safe disposal of excess runoff.

4. The proportion of time that the local extensionist can spend with farmers is greatly increased when the clients are located in groups rather than scattered throughout his or her district.

From a technical viewpoint, the topographic catchment may be best for planning, but the actual boundary of the local administrative unit (municipality, county, district, village leader's area, etc.) may in reality provide the most important social boundary within which to work. The involvement of the local community, its leaders, and government officials is usually essential for the widespread and lasting success of any rural development effort. Consequently, the local administrative unit may be preferable for social and political decisions, while subcatchments within this boundary may be the most appropriate for technical work and group action.

The land husbandry approach to achieving better production and conservation is equally applicable to administrative units and catchments, to large or small farms, and to scattered farms or consolidated groups of properties. The benefits to a community become most apparent when the improvements take place over significant contiguous areas of land, within small catchments in the administrative areas for local government.

Cross-slope Barriers Complement Good Land Husbandry

Need for Cross-slope Barriers. If unavoidable runoff is expected to occur on occasion, physical works in the form of cross-slope barriers are appropriate to control its movement and limit its erosive capacity. But all mechanical works and physical structures should be used to support and reinforce the main thrust of avoiding soil damage through good land husbandry.

Good soil cover by crops and residues act against both rainfall and runoff, while cross-slope barriers on the land surface, having no extra effect against rainfall, act only against runoff. This highlights again the prior and primary importance of good husbandry of crops and soil in achieving effective conservation.

Slope Length. The prime purpose of any cross-slope barrier is to divide the natural length of a hillside slope into shorter sections. This limits the volume and velocity of runoff that each structure must contain or guide. A

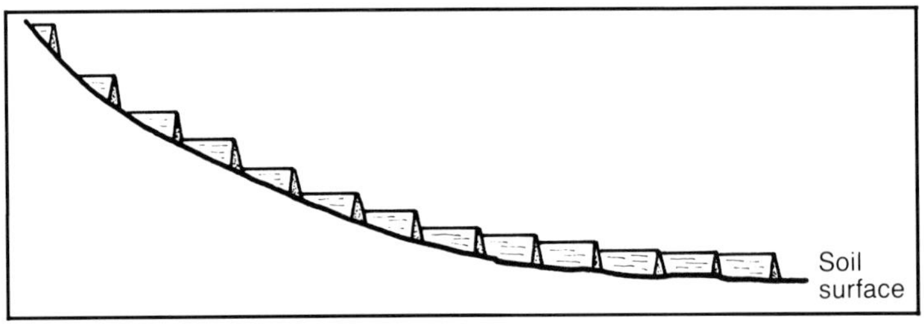

Figure 11. Slope steepness affects water detention capacity of regularly spaced cross-slope barriers.

Soil surface

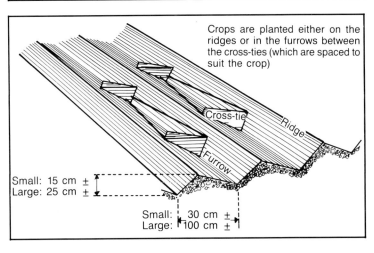

Crops are planted either on the ridges or in the furrows between the cross-ties (which are spaced to suit the crop)

Cross-tie

Ridge

Furrow

Small: 15 cm ±
Large: 25 cm ±

Small: 30 cm ±
Large: 100 cm ±

Figure 12. Detention storage provided by cross-ties in a ridge-and-furrow system.

Contour tillage causes cross-slope roughness that encourages infiltration of rainwater.

reduction in slope length reduces the chance of runoff gathering into constricted flow lines and so reduces the probability of rills and gullies forming.

Slope Steepness. Slope steepness is an important consideration because it affects the ease of contour tillage. It also affects the downslope velocity of runoff and, hence, its capacity to scour and transport soil. In addition, steepness affects the volume of water that can be detained by a given height of cross-slope barrier (Figure 11).

Importance of Contour Planting. Planting of crops, grasses, or trees up-and-down slope should always be avoided because of the tendency for runoff to become concentrated in the interrows, which increases its velocity and erosiveness. Where planting is done on the contour, tillage, weeding, and other operations tend to produce small banks and ridges that impede the downslope flow of water. This gives the water more time to soak in. A similar effect can be achieved by planting crops in a ridge-and-furrow system with cross-ties (Figure 12).

Types of Barriers. At the earliest stage of planning a layout of cross-slope barriers, one must decide what their purpose is to be. Their type, size, and spacing can then be designed accordingly.

Where the purpose is to detain all runoff until it has had time to soak in, impermeable barriers of appropriate size are set out on the contour. These can be either continuous or discontinuous across the slope.

This kind of barrier can only be constructed safely on deep soils with high permeability and high water storage capacity. On steep slopes with shallow soils and soils with relatively impermeable subsurface layers, the

A contoured ridge-and-furrow system on a slight gradient with cross-ties to trap rainwater. The system is also designed to allow any excess water to move slowly along the contour toward the drainage line.

accumulation of water in the profile may increase the risk of mass slippage. Good husbandry—promoting dense crop cover—can diminish this risk by favoring high evapotranspiration.

There are two other situations where trying to eliminate runoff may be undesirable: (1) where the crop needs drainage (for example, yams and tobacco) and (2) where the soil is shallow and cannot absorb all of the rain in a typical storm.

Where the purpose is to disperse and temporarily slow the velocity of runoff, permeable barriers of stones, trash lines of crop residues and weeds, or strips of closely spaced stems of grasses and other suitable plants are set out on the contour. These barriers also detain eroded soil and plant residues transported by runoff. On slopes of less than two percent, where the topography is fairly even, well-managed systems of such filter strips may be all that is needed for effective control of erosive flooding by runoff. In other situations, filter strips may provide the start of a system of progressive terracing.

Where the purpose is to carry runoff away, impermeable barriers are set out on gentle gradients across the slope to guide the runoff to suitable discharge points.

Controlling Runoff Velocity. For a given rate of runoff on a given slope steepness, a wider and more shallow flow will have less velocity (and, consequently, less erosive and transport capacity) than a narrow, deep flow because of the effects of frictional drag between the flowing water and the surface over which it flows. Velocity will also be reduced if the channel surface is rough, providing more frictional drag on the water. If other factors are the same, velocity will be slower on a shallow slope than a steep one. The safe design of channels to conduct runoff water relies on achieving a suitable combination of shape, erosion resistance, and gradient.

Channels to conduct runoff at controlled gradients across cultivated land are usually designed for bare-earth conditions. Channels of downslope waterways are generally protected by close-grown grasses or nonbiological materials, such as stones or concrete.

Types of Structures

It is essential to define the objective before considering which type of structure to use. First, any protection works must be appropriate for the intended crops. A system may be excellent for tree crops but unsuitable for annual crops. Second, the system must suit local conditions. Soil depth and rainfall determine whether a maximum infiltration scheme is practical or whether surface runoff must be managed. It is more important to understand the principles and how they can be applied to particular conditions than to follow even the best instruction manuals.

All cross-slope structures to control runoff on cropland are variations on two main forms: (1) bench-type terraces, where the area under the main crop is concentrated on the benches themselves, and (2) conservation banks, where most or all of the area under the main crop is in the spaces between the structures (Figure 13, Table 2).

Figure 13. Types and characteristics of bench terraces and conservation banks.

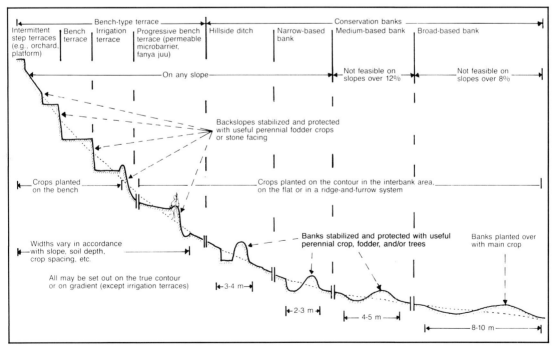

Both types may be designed and constructed either for retention of runoff, that is aligned on the true contour, or for safe discharge of runoff when aligned on gentle cross-slope gradients. Where the structures are aligned on a gradient, the watercourses into which they discharge must be of sufficient size, shape, and strength of lining to avoid erosion by peak flows.

Bench Terraces. Bench terraces can be used on any slope, from the steepest to the slightest. However, the effort needed to construct them is considerable, so they are generally used on steep slopes where other measures are unlikely to be effective. Maximum control of runoff and erosion is achieved when an entire hillslope is terraced and cropped. Terraces set out at intervals (intermittent terracing) require less soil moving and may be suitable for less intensive use, such as tree crops.

Bench terraces are normally constructed by cutting and filling to produce a series of level or nearly level steps or benches. To retain more rainfall, bench terraces may be inward-sloping (into the hillside) or level with a retaining bank on the forward edge. Terraces with an outward-sloping bench are common along the foothills of the Himalaya mountain range from Kashmir to Bhutan. They

Table 2. Features of bench terraces and conservation banks.

	What the Structure Does									
	Soil Management			Runoff Management				Cropping Pattern		
Type of Structure	Reduce Slope Percent	Reduce Slope Length	Trap Sediment	Retain All Runoff	Retain Part of Runoff	Disperse	Drainage*	Cropping on Structures	Cropping Between Structures	Typical Crop or Use
Bench terraces										
For annual crops										
Level	+	+		+				+		Any annual
Inward sloping	+	+		+				+		crops
Outward sloping	+	+			+			+		
Irrigation	+	+						+		
For perennial crops										
Step terraces	+	+		+	+			+		Tea, coffee,
Orchard terraces	+	+			+			+		rubber,
Platforms	+				+			+		fruit, oil palm
Developed progressively										
Fanya juu	+		+		+	+		+	+	Any crop
Stone walls	+		+		+	+			+	
Contour lines										
of vegetation †	+		+		+	+			+	
Conservation banks										
Stormwater drain										Above arable
or interception ditch ‡		+					+			land
Graded channel terrace										Arable land
or contour bank										
Narrow-based		+					+		+	
Broad-based		+					+	+		
Hillside ditch		+	+	+ or	+	or	+		+	Non-arable
Lock & spill drains					+				+	land
Retention banks										
Contour bund		+	+		+				+	
Murundum		+	+	+					+	
Trash lines		+	+		+	+			+	

*Drainage or dispersal of runoff for erosion control, or crop requirement, or water harvesting.
†Also called permeable microbarriers.
‡Also called storm drain, diversion terrace, interception channel.

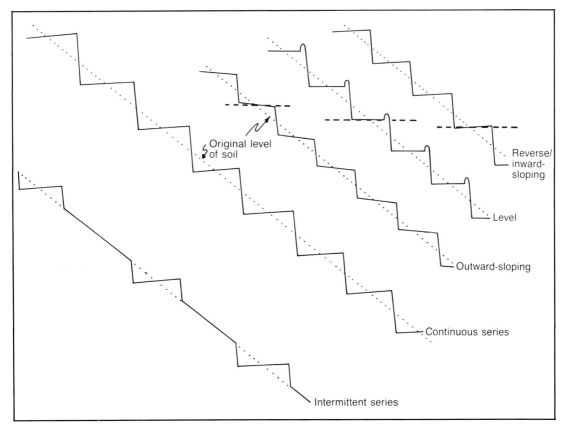

Original level of soil

Reverse/inward-sloping

Level

Outward-sloping

Continuous series

Intermittent series

Figure 14. Bench terraces.

reduce the slope steepness over the width of the bench and so reduce soil movement, but less runoff is retained than by level or inward-sloping benches (Figures 14 and 15). This may be desirable on steep slopes with shallow soils because too much water in the soil increases the risk of landslides.

Bench terraces usually are set out on a true contour, but may be constructed with a slight gradient along their length so that excess runoff flows to a discharge point. Irrigation terraces are bench terraces with arrangements for the control of irrigation water onto and along the terraces.

Size and Shape of Terraces. The width of the terraces and the spacing between them depend on several factors. A farmer usually prefers a wide terrace, especially when annual crops are grown with cultivation by animals or machines. But the wider the bench, the more earth must be moved. When cutting bench terraces, it is undesirable to expose subsoil or bedrock, so the maximum practical width is influenced by the depth of soil and slope of the land. A deep soil allows terraces to be wider and farther apart. As a guide, the vertical interval should not be more than two and one-half times the usable soil depth. For a given soil depth, a gentle slope allows wider terraces than a steep slope.

The riser or backslope is the ground between the level terraces. Sometimes, it is used to plant perennial grasses for animal feed. But usually it is regarded as unproductive land, and the farmer wishes to make it as small as possible. An unprotected steep slope is vulnerable to erosion, but it may be protected by planting perennial plants or strengthening the riser with stones cleared from the field surface to ease cultivation.

Bench Terracing for Perennial Crops. Special forms of bench terracing are used for perennial tree crops. For small bush crops, the terraces may be small and closely spaced, just wide enough for a single row of bushes on each terrace. Construction requires less labor than wider terraces and can be applied on steep slopes. This type, called step terracing, is particularly suitable for tea and coffee.

For larger tree crops, such as fruit and rubber, a wider spacing is required, and terraces are cut at intervals down the slope. Typical spacing might be 5 meters for fruit trees and 10 meters for rubber trees. Usually called orchard terraces, a single line of trees is planted on each terrace; the land between the terraces must be protected by a dense

Hillside ditch   Individual platform terrace

Orchard terrace

Intermittent terrace

Orchard terrace

Figure 15. Hillside ditch, individual platform terraces, and orchard terraces (from Peace Corps reprint R-62).

LAND HUSBANDRY

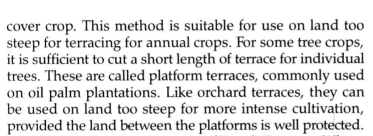

Bench terraces for tea protected by grass facing (left), and stone walling (above).

cover crop. This method is suitable for use on land too steep for terracing for annual crops. For some tree crops, it is sufficient to cut a short length of terrace for individual trees. These are called platform terraces, commonly used on oil palm plantations. Like orchard terraces, they can be used on land too steep for more intense cultivation, provided the land between the platforms is well protected.

Progressive Development of Bench Terraces. Where the labor or money required for building bench terraces is lacking, such terraces can be formed progressively over time by trapping soil that has been moved downhill by tillage and erosion. This is done by constructing barriers across the slope at intervals. The system does not have the immediate effect of formally constructed terraces, but it is much less laborious.

On gentle slopes, permeable microbarriers are made on the contour using lines of stones, crop residues, grass, or shrubs (Figure 16). On steeper slopes, banks of earth or fitted stones are used (Figures 17 and 18). The "fanya juu" type (meaning "throw upwards") of earth bank developed in Kenya is effective, as are the "fosses aveugles," or blind ditches, developed by Belgian conservationists in Rwanda-Burundi.

Each bank then forms the backslope of the terrace below, and it is built up by adding soil from below the bank or by putting on more stones or planting more grass, shrubs, or trees over several seasons. As with bench terraces constructed in a single operation, stones cleared from cultivated areas or useful perennial plants can be used to protect the backslopes.

Another advantage of forming terraces progressively is that they can begin with a wide spacing; more banks can then be put in later, halfway between the original banks.

Runoff may flow downslope over the lip of the terrace. This may be acceptable so long as (a) the runoff moves across a wide, shallow front and is not concentrated in erosive channels and (b) the front slope of the terrace is sufficiently protected by grass or stones to withstand the runoff that flows down it.

Soil moisture will be more abundant near the banks of such terraces than in the intervening areas until the terrace is finally shaped by the farmer into a level bench, or has been treated with a cross-tied, ridge-and-furrow water-detention system.

Conservation Banks. There are many forms and types of conservation banks; in some cases there are alternative names for the same structure. When considering the use of this type of protection, the important thing is to be clear about the exact purpose. They are all directed toward managing runoff in some ways, but they may be intended to:

▶ Retain or detain runoff to encourage infiltration.

▶ Disperse runoff into thin, nonerosive flows and prevent it from concentrating in rills or gullies.

▶ Guide runoff across the slope to a discharge point.

Conservation banks are set up intermittently down a slope, so the reduction in the rate of runoff and soil loss is generally less than that achieved by bench terraces. Banks are thus less efficient than bench terraces, but they are also much less laborious and costly to construct.

In deciding what type of conservation banks to con-

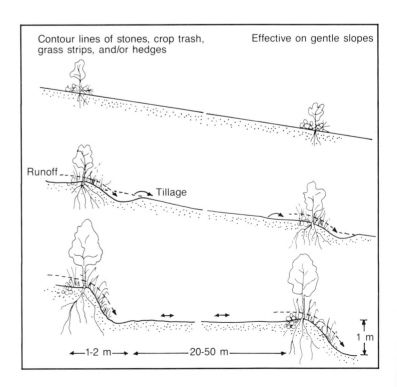

Figure 16. Progressive formation of bench terraces: permeable microbarriers.

Contour lines of stones, crop trash, grass strips, and/or hedges

Effective on gentle slopes

Runoff

Tillage

1-2 m

20-50 m

1 m

LAND HUSBANDRY

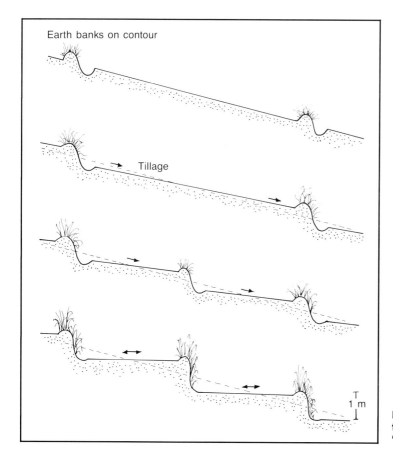

Earth banks on contour

Tillage

1 m

Figure 17. Progressive formation of bench terraces: "fanya juu" banks.

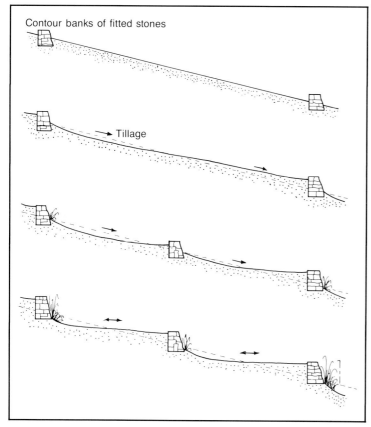

Contour banks of fitted stones

Tillage

Figure 18. Progressive formation of bench terraces: stone banks.

struct, land slope, type of farming, and available means of constructing the banks must be considered. The more rain that infiltrates into the soil during rainstorms, the less the runoff per unit area, so conservation banks can be smaller or spaced further apart.

Again, good husbandry of crops and soil is a key feature in achieving conservation and in reducing the costs of doing so.

The design of the various forms is based on well-established hydrologic and hydraulic principles, which are described in the textbooks and manuals listed in the bibliography of this publication.

Stormwater Diversion Drains. These drains are also known as cutoff drains or interception ditches. The purpose is to intercept or divert surface runoff from higher ground when it is necessary to keep it off lower land, such as arable fields. In form, the drain is an open channel with

Progressive formation of bench terraces. A trash line holds the soil while letting runoff pass.

Lessening of usable slope on benches forming between grass lines on the contour.

a bank on the downhill side. The design is complex and consists of estimating the maximum rate of flow the channel may have to carry, then chosing a suitable combination of size, shape, channel roughness, and gradient that will lead the runoff away at a safe velocity.

Structures designed to carry away surplus runoff should not have their channels clogged with eroded soil. To prevent this from happening in situations where runoff is also carrying eroded soil, filter strips of close-growing grasses can be planted on the uphill edge of the channels to trap the soil and to let the water pass into the channel. This is seldom done, however, and the channels may become choked with sediment, thereby increasing the danger of overtopping and breakage of the banks, followed by downslope gullying. Frequent and careful maintenance is therefore needed if conservation banks to carry runoff are to function as designed.

Contour Banks or Graded Channel Terraces. Contour banks or graded channel terraces serve a similar function on arable fields: they interrupt downhill runoff and lead it away to a safe discharge. They are similar in shape to diversion drains, but smaller because they carry a smaller flow. The design features are the distance between banks down the slope and the size, shape, and gradient of the channel. Design manuals give standard designs for different situations based on field experience.

On gentle slopes (less than eight percent) under mechanized arable farming, the banks are built low and wide, constructed by earth-moving machinery. They can be planted over with the main crop and crossed by farm machinery. On steeper slopes the banks are built narrower and higher, with steep sides, and they cannot be crossed by farm machinery. They can be constructed with common farm plows or sets of disks, or with larger mechanized equipment, such as bulldozers and road graders. If banks are large and their side-slopes steep, only the latter types of equipment are appropriate for construction.

Hillside Ditches The hillside ditch is another practice used on slopes too steep for bench terracing. The term is applied to several shapes, the common feature being a ditch dug on the contour to catch soil and water. There may also be a small terrace either level or inward-sloping. A variation is the lock-and-spill drain, where low cross-walls divide the drain bed into separate basins (locks) to encourage infiltration. In heavy rains the runoff overtops these cross-walls and spills toward the discharge outlet.

Retention Banks. Such banks are conservation banks whose primary purpose is to retain runoff to increase infiltration. In Brazil, large banks, called murundums, are built by earth-moving machinery with the intention of catching and holding all the runoff, even in torrential storms. This approach is only practical on deep soils with

A small broad-based bank used as a field road in Kasungu, Malawi.

This "murundum" in Parana, Brazil, is another form of a broad-based bank on the level contour.

A narrow-based bank, Jaipur, India.

LAND HUSBANDRY

high moisture storage capacity. Similar but smaller retention banks called contour bunds are used in India, usually with an emergency overflow that operates like a dam spillway in extreme storms.

Permeable barriers may be used to detain surface runoff temporarily to encourage infiltration and to disperse runoff that tends to concentrate in rills or depressions by allowing it to percolate more uniformly through the barrier. The barriers may be formed by planting rows of grasses or shrubs, by placing lines of stones along the contour, or by piling crop residues and weeds into rows on the contour, when they are called trash lines. The barriers may also be intended to trap sediment to improve plant growth on the upstream side of the barriers.

Permeable barriers are particularly useful on gentle slopes in semiarid areas where the main effect is to improve the water retention. On steep lands, planted rows of grass and shrubs are commonly used, in particular ipil-ipil (*Leucaena leucocephala*), elephant grass (*Pennisetum purpureum*), vetiver grass (*Vetiveria zizanoides*), and other grasses that form a dense root system. Contour lines of such grasses can reduce runoff and erosion and, by trapping sediment, reduce the effective slope of the cultivated land between the strips.

The better topsoil conditions and infiltration are maintained, the further apart conservation banks can be spaced for a given size of structure, or the smaller they can be at a given spacing.

Safe Waterways. Where unavoidable runoff runs into a water course or is conducted there by gradient terraces, the runoff may have sufficient energy to damage the bed of the waterway. This can be avoided by ensuring that the size, shape, and lining of the waterway is adequate to conduct safely the expected maximum flow.

Because the amount of runoff from a cultivated catchment served by a waterway is probably greater than it was before cultivation, the natural condition of the channel

Figure 19. Stepped waterway on a steep slope.

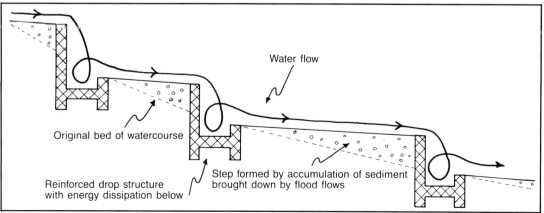

Water flow

Original bed of watercourse

Reinforced drop structure with energy dissipation below

Step formed by accumulation of sediment brought down by flood flows

shape and lining may prove insufficient to accommodate the flow after cultivation. Scouring may result.

Observation of the slope, shape, soil types, and type and condition of the channel's lining permit calculations to be made of the channel's capacity. Calculation of the runoff expected from the contributing catchment then permits an estimate of what improvements in shape or lining are needed to allow it to conduct the maximum flow without damage.

The channel lining can be strengthened to resist the effects of fast-flowing water with suitable grass cover or some nonliving lining, such as stones or concrete.

The cross-sectional shape of the waterway can be made wider and shallower so as to spread the flow in a

A gabion "drop structure" (right) stabilizing a streambed. The apron below the structure breaks the force of falling water. A good stone/grass lining (below) in a waterway can permit runoff to flow at high speeds without eroding the soil.

Young tea planted in a ridge-and-furrow system, with inter-row mulching, narrow-based banks planted with Eragrostis for mulch, and a grassed waterway. This hierarchy of catchments is at Lujer, Malawi.

broad and relatively slow-flowing sheet all across its width to reduce the risk of scour. The more resistant the ultimate waterway lining, the higher the velocities it can safely sustain and the narrower the waterway can safely be. Waterways must always be maintained to their design specifications. If they are not, there is a serious risk of them becoming gullies.

Where a preferred combination of slope, cross-sectional shape, and lining of a watercourse is still insufficient to allow any of the above adjustments to operate safely, another recourse is to use a series of drop structures. These break the slope along the length of the waterway into a series of steps between which wide but shallow slopes are maintained and suitably protected. The runoff falls in sequence over the drop structures, which are designed to fortify the lip of the step and to dissipate the falling water's energy before flowing again at shallow gradient downslope to the next step. Steep watercourses can be stablized in this manner, but require careful maintenance if they are to remain effective (Figure 19). The cost of building the necessary structures is high, which often inhibits their construction.

Where the watercourse joins the stream or river, a gully may start and work its way back up the waterway. An adequate drop structure at this critical point may be essential to prevent this from happening.

A Hierarchy of Catchments

The total catchment of any stream or river is formed by collections of lesser catchments, whether the land use is crops, pasture, forest, or a mixture of several uses:

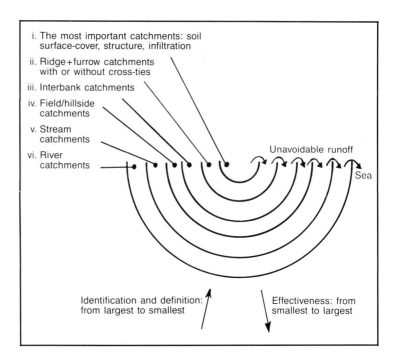

i. The most important catchments: soil surface-cover, structure, infiltration
ii. Ridge+furrow catchments with or without cross-ties
iii. Interbank catchments
iv. Field/hillside catchments
v. Stream catchments
vi. River catchments

Unavoidable runoff

Sea

Identification and definition: from largest to smallest

Effectiveness: from smallest to largest

Figure 20. A hierachy of "nested" catchments.

1. The smallest catchments formed by the roughness and good structure of every square centimeter of soil.

2. The microcatchments formed by cross-tied ridges and furrows, if these have been installed.

3. The interbank catchments, between pairs of bench terraces or conservation banks, if these have been installed.

4. The field and hillside catchments, comprised of the total group of lesser catchments.

5. The river catchment formed by the sum of its tributary stream catchments.

In the identification and definition of these "nested" catchments—using maps, airphotos, and on-the-ground surveys—work starts with the largest units and progresses toward the smallest. However, the effectiveness of the system in catching rainwater where it falls and then safely infiltrating or disposing of the excess progresses in the reverse order, from the smallest to the largest (Figure 20).

HOW TO PROCEED

If you find yourself in charge of initiating a project for soil and water conservation on erodible land, the following are considerations that experience has shown to be helpful, if not essential, to ensure success.

1. Set up an office that has the following, in addition to normal secretarial and drafting facilities, equipment, and operating expenses:
   a. A big table on which to lay out maps.
   b. Maps and airphotos of your region.
   c. Adequate means of storing and indexing maps and the information derived from them.
   d. Sufficient and adequate (but not excessively sophisticated) equipment to view stereopairs of airphotos.
   e. Adequate, simple equipment for assessing essential land and soil characteristics, such as soil augers, clinometer, compass, and pH kit.
   f. Technical manuals on agriculture, land husbandry, and soil and water conservation applicable to your region.
   g. Suitable means of transportation for fieldwork and funding for its operation and repair.

2. Study all currently available information about your area to start building up a baseline inventory of natural resources and current land use; the inventory will serve as a basis for developing strategies for improved use and management of land resources:
   a. What the general area and specific catchments within it look like (airphotos, maps of soils, topography, lithology, vegetation, climate, land uses, soil survey reports, etc.) as a guide to understanding the agroecological situation.
   b. What land use systems prevail in the area; how plant and animal production systems interact; how they function over the annual climatic cycle; how problems of runoff and erosion relate to tillage and other land use practices; and how they may have changed or been amended over the years (reports from extension, studies by other entities, etc.)

   c. What is the present socioeconomic situation of the people in terms of customs, attitudes, availability of inputs, marketing, net incomes, etc. (reports from extension and other entities, etc.).

3. Arrange to fill in important gaps in any of the above information that will be needed when discussing, deciding upon, and planning appropriate activities with the people of the area.

4. Undertake appropriate field surveys to supply the missing information (or if the information cannot be obtained, decide how best to proceed without it).

5. With the people of the area, identify, discuss, and rank the greatest problems and potentials, then decide which ones are feasible to tackle or to develop.

6. Search for possible means of solving the problems or realizing the potentials among researchers, extension workers, and technical reports in the agroecological and socioeconomic fields.

7. If such information does not exist, press for its provision by appropriate people or organizations as soon as possible.

8. Discuss with the community and farmers and jointly decide upon the types, sequences, and rates of action that are adequate, appropriate, feasible, and acceptable.

9. Make suitable joint arrangements for action to start work, such as:
   a. Leadership, both of community groups and of technical and administrative staff.
   b. Technical advice and assistance.
   c. Financial resources.
   d. Supply of farm inputs.
   e. Processing, disposal, and use of farm outputs.

10. Work with the people in implementing the chosen program.

Photo Credits